Contents

Read This before You Start 4

Introduction to Astronomy 5

Sun, Moon, and Earth 5
From Mercury to Pluto 8
Cosmic Bolts of Light—the
  "Shooting Stars" 8
The Fixed Stars: Beacons in
  Outer Space 9
The Constellations 10
The Ecliptic and the
  Zodiac 11
Looking for the Limits of the
  Universe: The Milky Way
  and Other Galaxies 12
Table of Planets and Fixed
  Stars 14

**The Star Maps and How to
Use Them** 15

What Do the Star Maps
  Show? 15
How Do I Use the Maps? 16
Where Do the Maps
  Apply? 17
For What Times Are the
  Maps Valid? 17
When and Where Can One
  See the Planets? 18
Table of the Lunar Phases 20

Star Map Series N I 21

Geographical Map 21
Star Maps N I 22–33
Andromeda 34

Boötes and Corona
  Borealis 35
Ursa Major and Canes
  Venatici 36
Ursa Minor and Draco 37
Auriga 38
Leo 39
Perseus 40

Star Map Series N II 41

Geographical Map 41
Star Maps N II 42–53
Aquila 54
Canis Major and Lepus 55
Virgo, Corvus, Libra 56
Cancer and Gemini 57
Orion and Canis Minor 58
Cygnus and Lyra 59
Aries and Taurus 60

Star Map Series S 61

Geographical Map 61
Star Maps S 62–73
Eridanus 74
Dorado 75
Southern Cross and
  Centaurus 76
Carina and Musca 77
Hydrus and Tucana 78
Scorpius and Corona
  Australis 79
Table for Finding the Correct
  Star Map on inside
  back cover

S0-AAZ-768

Read This before You Start

Many people have become interested in astronomy because of the spectacular accomplishments of modern space exploration and because of fascinating celestial events like solar and lunar eclipses. In regions where the air is clear and unpolluted—as in the mountains—and in southern countries, the multitude of stars can often seem so overwhelming that one finds oneself wondering how anyone knows what is what in the night sky.

With this new Barron's Mini Fact Finder *Stars: June 1992–May 1995 Edition*, you will be able to orient yourself quickly and easily. In it there are 56 maps that show all the stars, constellations, and planets that are visible in different seasons and at different nighttime hours from almost any point on Earth. Whatever continent you may be on, with the help of this pocket-sized guide you will be able to figure out anywhere and at any hour of the night what part of the sky you are seeing.

The "Introduction to Astronomy" (see page 5) gives you a basic understanding of the amazing interplay between the celestial bodies.

This 1992–1995 edition includes the following features:

- Dates of interest for the years 1992, 1993, 1994, and 1995.
- A table of the lunar phases (page 20) that gives the dates of all the phases: full moon and new moon as well as first quarter and last quarter.
- The spectacular eclipsing of the bright planets by the moon, which occasionally conceals even the distant planets. Each of these rare events, if it is visible in the evening until about two hours after sunset, is mentioned in connection with the relevant star maps.

A special advantage of this guide is that it fits into any shirt or trouser pocket. This makes it especially suitable for travelers, who will now be able to find the answer to questions concerning the night sky in whatever country they are.

The author and the editors of Barron's Mini Fact Finders wish you much enjoyment and success in exploring the night sky.

The photo on the preceding double page depicts the Milky Way in the area of Sagittarius, where there are hundreds of thousands of stars. Interspersed among the stars is gas in huge masses that are made to glow by the stars. The Lagoon Nebula (dark red) and the Trifid Nebula (red and blue) are among the most beautiful nebulae.

Introduction to Astronomy

Sun, Moon, and Earth

For us, Earth is the most important celestial body. Earth is a spherical object 7,913 miles (12,742 km) in diameter and enveloped by a layer of air (the atmosphere) that, by protecting us from dangerous cosmic radiation, makes life possible for us. Once a day, that is, every 24 hours, Earth rotates around its own axis, which is an imaginary straight line that runs from the north to the south pole. Because of Earth's rotation we see the stars rise in the east and set in the west. In the course of the night the starry sky changes its appearance completely: New stars appear, and others vanish from sight.

The sun is crucial for Earth and its inhabitants. It is a huge, blazing ball of gas, in whose core atomic nuclei are fused in a process that releases energy. Thanks to the incredibly vast amounts of energy thus produced, the sun radiates great quantities of light and heat toward Earth and thus provides the energy that is necessary for any kind of life to emerge. The rising and setting of the sun create our days and nights.

When the sun is in the sky during the day, it shines so brightly that all other celestial bodies—that are overhead not just at night but during the day as well—fade from sight. It is only in the evening, when the sun sinks below the horizon and darkness falls, that we can see the other, much less luminous celestial bodies.

The sun's disk frequently displays dark spots. The number of these so-called sunspots fluctuates in an eleven-year cycle. The "solar activity" associated with sunspots reached a maximum in 1991.

Only one other celestial body is sometimes visible during the day: the moon, which measures 2,159 miles (3,484 km) in diameter and is thus considerably smaller than Earth. The moon revolves around Earth approximately once a month. It is Earth's companion or satellite, a cold celestial body that is inhospitable to life. A human first set foot on the moon on July 20, 1969. Like Earth, the moon derives its light from the sun, and it reflects this light back to Earth. The moon appears to us in continually changing form as it circles around Earth; we speak of its "waxing" and "waning" as, in the course of 29 1/2 days, it passes through the different phases of the lunar cycle. The diagram below shows how these familiar "lunar phases" come about.

Depending on the moon's position in relation to the sun, we see sometimes the entire lit-up side of the moon (full moon); sometimes only half of the lit-up side (half moon); and, when the moon is closest to the sun, we don't see anything at all because the moon turns its unlit side toward us (new moon). A table of the lunar phases is given on page 20.

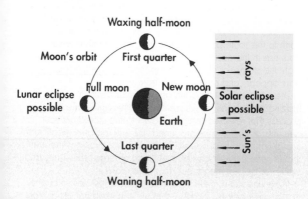

As it revolves around Earth, the moon occasionally produces the most dramatic celestial events we can observe: lunar and solar eclipses. The diagram below shows how eclipses come about. Earth and the moon throw shadows, like any other body that is lit up. When Earth's shadow falls on the moon, we see a lunar eclipse; when the moon's shadow hits Earth, it causes a solar eclipse. Solar eclipses are always visible from only a small part of Earth's surface; lunar eclipses, on the other hand,

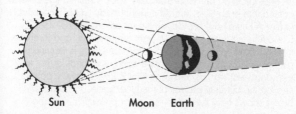

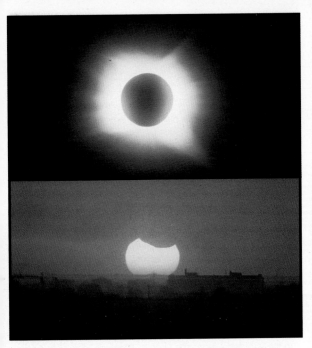

Total solar eclipses like the one that occurred on June 11, 1983 (above), are especially impressive. This eclipse was visible in Indonesia. The dark disk of the moon is directly in front of the sun and blocks all its light. In a partial solar eclipse (below) only part of the sun's disk is covered by the moon. On July 20, 1982, the sun disappeared below the horizon in Hamburg, Germany during such a partial eclipse.

can be seen on about half of Earth's night side. Both lunar and solar eclipses can be total or partial depending on whether the solar or lunar disk is entirely covered up or only partially covered. In a total solar eclipse we can see the sun's corona for a few minutes. This ring of radiating light consists of highly diffused gases heated to a temperature of several million degrees Celsius, but its luminosity is too slight to be seen except during total eclipses.

Solar and lunar eclipses are quite rare, and they are not visible from all parts of Earth. All eclipses from June, 1992 through May, 1995 both solar and lunar, are briefly described in the text accompanying the star maps.

From Mercury to Pluto

Earth not only rotates around its axis every 24 hours; it also circles around the sun, completing one orbit in exactly one year. But it is not alone on this journey; eight other "planets" (from a Greek word for "wanderer") also revolve around the central body of what we call our solar system. The planets, listed in order of increasing distance from the sun, are: Mercury, Venus, Earth, Mars, Jupiter, Saturn, Uranus, Neptune, and Pluto. The following mnemonic sentence will help you remember their order: My Very Eager Mother Just Spotted Umpteen New Planets.

The planets differ greatly from each other. Some are considerably larger than Earth, like Jupiter, the biggest of the planets. Some are much hotter, like Mercury, whose proximity to the sun exposes it to the full force of the sun's rays, giving it a surface temperature of 400 degrees Celsius. On some planets it is very cold, as on Pluto, which is 3.6 billion miles (5.9 billion km) from the sun—that is 40 times the distance between Earth and the sun. On Pluto the temperature reaches a low of minus 230 degrees Celsius. Of the nine planets only five are visible to the unaided eye; to see Uranus, Neptune, and Pluto a telescope is needed. The same is true for the impressive rings of Saturn (see page 9) and for the asteroids or "minor planets," which orbit around the sun by the thousands.

Cosmic Bolts of Light—the "Shooting Stars"

Often during a clear night what we call meteors or shooting stars streak briefly across the sky. These bright and sometimes startling trails of light that spurt at lightning speed are caused by tiny metallic and rock particles that enter Earth's atmosphere from outer space. The particles become extremely hot, excite the air to incandescence with their great speed, and are incinerated completely in the process. A grain of dust weighing less than one gram can become a meteor that momentarily glows brighter than the brightest stars.

This is what the planet Saturn looks like from a distance of 11 million miles (18 million km) as recorded by the cameras of Voyager I on October 30, 1980. The shadow that Saturn's rings cast onto the planet's surface is 62,000 miles (100,000 km) wide at the middle. The rings are composed of billions of small dust and ice particles that orbit around the planet.

The Fixed Stars: Beacons in Outer Space

If one looks at the sky on a clear night and far from the air pollution of cities, one has the impression of seeing innumerable stars. In fact, "only" about 2,500 stars are visible to the naked eye. When one looks through binoculars or a telescope, the number of visible stars increases to hundreds of thousands or several million. All the stars rise and set in the sky just like the sun, moon, and planets, because Earth rotates around itself once a day. Apart from this nightly rising and setting, the stars exhibit practically no motion; their position in relation to each other remains essentially constant. Because of this apparent immobility the astronomers of antiquity called them the "fixed stars."

The reason the stars seem to be glued to their places in the sky is that they are separated from Earth by incredibly vast distances. To illustrate how distance affects our perception of the speed of motion we need only think of a train passing us on the ground and an airplane flying high in the sky overhead. The train seems to move much faster, in spite of the fact that the airplane's speed exceeds that of the train by several hundred miles per hour.

The stars are so very far removed from Earth that astronomers had to invent a new unit for measuring distance, the light-year.

One light-year is the distance that light travels (at a speed per second of 186,282 miles or 300,000 km, a distance equal to 7 1/2 times around Earth's equator) in exactly one year. It is equivalent to 5.86 trillion miles (9.46 trillion km). (A trillion is a "1" followed by 12 zeroes.)

How is it possible for us to see stars at all at such incredible, "astronomical" distances? Because they emit huge amounts of heat and light, just like our sun. All fixed stars are suns, some bigger, some smaller than ours.

Fixed stars and planets are therefore two entirely different things. Stars are spheres of incandescent gas that produce their own light; the planets are solid, cold bodies that orbit around the sun and are illuminated by it. The stars are light-years away from us—that is trillions of miles—while the planets move much closer to Earth, being separated from us by "mere" millions or billions of miles. The other big difference between stars and planets is that planets do not stay in one place in the sky. They revolve around the sun and thus keep changing their positions as seen from Earth, appearing now in one constellation, now in another.

The Constellations

According to a Greek myth, King Cepheus and Cassiopeia, his queen, once ruled over Ethiopia. Cassiopeia bragged one day that she was more beautiful than the goddesses, who were so incensed at this affront that they sent a sea monster to ravage Ethiopia. On advice of the priests the royal couple were about to sacrifice their daughter Andromeda to the monster to save their country, when, in the nick of time, Perseus arrived on the scene, killed the monster, and freed Andromeda. The gods later transported all participants in the drama to the heavens, where they can still be seen today as constellations, including even the sea monster in the shape of Cetus, the Whale.

This is just one of many stories told by ancient bards, stories whose characters the Greeks thought they recognized in the skies. These ancient people looked for bright stars and combined them in images that they then named after legendary celebrities. In the southern half of the celestial sphere, we find startlingly different names, such as Antlia, the Air Pump. Many of the southern constellations were not named until the eighteenth century, when astronomers no longer had much use for ancient mythology and preferred to elevate the most recent scientific inventions to the heavens—one of which was the air pump.

From a number of different traditions modern astronomers have selected a total of 88 constellations and drawn up internationally recognized boundaries between them. Of these 88 constellations the most obviously visible 57 appear in the star maps of this star guide. Each constellation has its own characteristic shape. Today the constellations no longer have meaning beyond orienting the observer of the starry sky; they constitute a kind of "coordinate grid" of the sky.

The Ecliptic and the Zodiac

There are twelve constellations that have a special importance: Aries, Taurus, Gemini, Cancer, Leo, Virgo, Libra, Scorpius, Sagittarius, Capricorn, Aquarius, and Pisces—the constellations of the zodiac. Through these constellations runs one of the most important (imaginary) lines used in astronomy as an orientation aid, namely the "ecliptic." The ecliptic is the circle the sun seems to describe around the celestial sphere in the course of a year. In reality it is, of course, Earth that circles around the sun once a year, not the the sun around Earth. But the only way to observe Earth's movement around the sun would be from a point outside the solar system. When we look at the sun from where we are, it seems as though the sun travels along the celestial sphere. This apparent journey takes the sun through the constellations of the zodiac, precisely along the line of the ecliptic. It is because of the sun's apparent movement that some constellations are visible only during the summer and others only during winter. Thus, when the sun is in front of Leo's stars, this constellation rises in the morning along with the sun. All the stars in and around Leo travel across the sky along with the sun during the day. We cannot see them because the sun's brilliant light obliterates the more modest gleam of the stars. In the evening Leo's stars drop below the western horizon along with the sun and are thus not visible during the night either. Not until six months later, when the sun has moved away from Leo and is on the opposite side of the sky in the constellation Capricorn, do Leo and its neighbors rise in the east as the sun sets in the west, and now we can watch them in the night sky. Because the sun repeats its apparent journey annually with great precision, every year we see the same stars and constellations at any given month or day.

The moon and all the planets also move along the ecliptic. The ecliptic is also therefore important in watching these celestial bodies. They appear to us always only along this imagined line, that is, in front of the zodiacal constellations. (The phrase "in front of" literally refers to a spatial relationship, for the planets, as we have already seen, are only millions or at most a few billion miles away from us, whereas the fixed stars are many trillions of miles distant.)

The names of the zodiacal constellations (such as Aries, Taurus, and Gemini) may be familiar to you from horoscopes; you were born under one of these "signs." We will not further discuss astrological signs in this star guide because, except for their names, they have nothing in common with the *constellations* of the zodiac (see page 79).

Looking for the Limits of the Universe: The Milky Way and Other Galaxies

One of the most imposing celestial sights is the Milky Way: It is a band of light produced by billions of stars. The single stars, if they each stood isolated in the sky, would be too faint to be seen, but all of them combine into a band of shimmering light. Interspersed among these billions of stars are clouds of dark dust that in places block the light from reaching Earth and give the Milky Way an uneven, ragged look. The universe includes more than the Milky Way; there are innumerable, similar formations in space that are made up of stars and dust and gases;

The Large Magellanic Cloud (LMC), along with the Small Magellanic Cloud (SMC), is among the galaxies that are closest to Earth.

each formation is a "galaxy" like our Milky Way. ("Galaxy" and "Milky Way" have the same meaning since *gala* is Greek for "milk.") All the galaxies together—most of them millions or billions of light-years away—make up the universe, for whose exploration astronomers today have a vast array of instruments at their disposal: There are not only sophisticated mirror and radio telescopes but also space vehicles ranging from satellites orbiting around Earth and observing objects beyond its atmosphere to space probes like Voyager II, which traveled as far as Jupiter, Saturn, Uranus, and Neptune in the course of its journey from 1977 to 1989.

Table of Planets and Fixed Stars

The Planets

Name	Distance from sun in mill. miles/(km)	Diameter miles/(km)	Mass*	Number of satellites
Mercury	36 (57.9)	3,006 (4,840)	.05	—
Venus	67.2 (108.2)	7,517 (12,104)	.81	—
Earth	92.9 (149.6)	7,913 (12,742)	1	1
Mars	141.5 (227.9)	4,219 (6,794)	.11	2
Jupiter	483 (778)	88,672 (142,790)	318	16
Saturn	886 (1,427)	74,520 (120,000)	95	18
Uranus	1,782 (2,870)	31,547 (50,800)	14	15
Neptune	2,792 (4,496)	30,180 (48,600)	17	8
Pluto	3,689 (5,940)	1,863 (3,000)	.002	1

*In multiples of Earth's mass: 1 = 5,976 quintillion tons

The Ten Brightest Stars

Name	Constellation	Distance from Earth (in light-years)	Mass*	Diameter (Multiple of sun's diam.)
(Sun)	—	(92.9 mill. miles/ 149.6 mill. km)	1	(.87 mill. m. /1.4 mill.km)
Sirius	Canis Major (see p. 55)	8.6	3	1.7
Canopus	Carina (see p. 77)	74	12	60
Toliman (Alpha Centauri)	Centaurus (see p. 76)	4.2	1	1
Vega	Lyra (see p. 59)	26	4	3
Capella	Auriga (see p. 38)	46	3	16
Arcturus	Boötes (see p.35)	36	4	26
Rigel	Orion (see p. 58)	1,300	30	19
Procyon	Canis Minor (see p. 58)	11	2	2
Achernar	Eridanus (see p. 74)	280	6	9
Altair	Aquila (see p. 54)	16	2	1.6

* Multiples of the sun's mass: 1 = 2,000 septillion tons

The Star Maps and How to Use Them

Astronomers have divided the celestial sphere that seems to surround us into two halves that are analogous to Earth's northern and southern hemispheres. There is also a celestial north and a celestial south pole—they lie on the extended axis that runs through Earth's north and south poles—and a celestial equator. Thus, just as we have northern and southern countries on Earth, there are northern and southern constellations in the sky. Only one half of the celestial sphere is visible from any one point on Earth; the other half lies below the circle of the horizon. Each star map shows the half of the sky that is visible from a particular place and at a particular time.

What Do the Star Maps Show?

All the maps show only "fixed" stars. These stars are classified into three groups according to their brightness: The faintest are represented by the smallest dots, the brightest, by the biggest. In the hazy skies lit up by city lights the brightest are practically the only stars one can detect, and they are also the ones that show up first as dusk falls. The names that appear in the round star maps are those of constellations, and the main stars making up a constellation are connected by lines so that the characteristic shapes of the constellations can be quickly identified (see inside front cover). Once you have gained an overview of the stars in the sky with the help of the round maps, you may want to find out a little more about some individual stars and constellations. That is why at the end of each map series the most important constellations are briefly presented. Here you will find the names of especially bright stars. To facilitate finding the constellations in the sky, the diagrams include directional arrows pointing to the celestial north pole (NP) or the celestial south pole (SP). The same letters also appear on the round maps so that you can look for the constellations in their proper positions. The ecliptic that appears in the round maps is only an imaginary line, but the maps show it as a line passing near certain bright stars to help you picture it in the sky. The Milky Way is represented by a whitish area, and its dark parts are also indicated.

How Do I Use the Maps?

If you face north (N), geographic east (E) lies on your right and geographic west (W) on your left. On the maps, east and west appear reversed. The reason for this is as follows: Each map shows the celestial hemisphere above you, and, in order to compare it to the stars overhead, you would have to hold it above your head. Try doing this once, making sure the N on the map points north. You will see that E and W point in the correct directions.

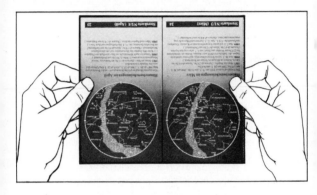

But in actual practice, reading star maps this way is very awkward, and the usual way is to hold the map vertically in front of you with the direction of the sky you want to observe pointing downward. Thus, if you want to watch the eastern sky, hold the map so that E is at the bottom, or, if you face north, N is at the bottom. You may be holding the book sideways or upside down (picture above), but what you see overhead exactly matches the part of the map above the letter indicating direction (as shown on inside front cover)—and that is what counts!

Determining the points of the compass is quite easy. In the northern hemisphere the Big Dipper and Polaris—the latter always glows in the north—help you get oriented (see page 37). How to find the south celestial pole in the southern hemisphere, where there is no polar star, is explained in connection with the map S/February (see page 70).

Where Do the Maps Apply?

What stars are visible depends (apart from the time of day and year) on the geographic latitude of the location from which you are observing the sky. In this *Star Guide* the views of the sky are grouped in three categories—one for 50 degrees north latitude (N I), one for 30 degrees north latitude (N II), and one for 20 degrees south latitude (S). Your point of observation may deviate from these meridians by as much as 10 degrees in either direction without the view of the sky changing significantly. This star guide thus can be used in almost all parts of the world. Just look in the geographical maps (page 21, 41, or 61) for the place where you are located.

For What Times Are the Maps Valid?

Each of the round star maps depicts the sky for the month given in big print at the bottom of the page. The sky is shown as it appears at 9:30 PM at the beginning of the month, at 8:30 PM in the middle of the month, and at 7:30 PM at the end of the month. You don't have to pay too close attention to the exact times; if you want to watch the stars anytime between 8 and 10 PM, just find the correct month given at the bottom of each map page.

In the countries that observe daylight saving time, the clocks are set ahead an hour for the period from April to October. The exact dates of the change are given under the relevant maps. For stargazing, the practical consequence of daylight saving time is that for the maps of series N I and N II the times of validity are shifted during the summer to 10:30 PM for the beginning, 9:30 PM for the middle, and 8:30 PM for the end of the month, that is, to between approximately 9 and 11 PM. In the southern hemisphere the seasons come at different times of the calendar year. When we have summer, it is winter there. If you plan to use the star maps of series S, you should inquire whether summer or winter time is in effect in the place where you wish to stargaze.

Keep in mind that the transitions from one month to the next are gradual. This is important especially for the last and very first days of the month. If, for instance, you want to identify stars at 11 PM on July 30, you should turn to the map for August, which applies for the beginning of August at 10:30 PM. Conversely, for watching the stars around 8:45 PM on May 3, the map for April is recommended, for it shows what the sky looks like at the end of April around 8:30 PM.

If you want to stargaze at a time of night other than between 8 and 10 PM (9 and 11 PM during daylight saving time), turn to the table on the inside back cover. Find the month you are interested in at the top and the hour of night in the left-hand column: Where the vertical and the horizontal lines intersect, you will be directed to the correct map to use.

Let us look at an example: You would like to watch the stars in Texas (the geographical map on page 41 shows that map series N II applies here) on July 10 at 1 AM. In July, daylight saving time is in effect. This means you have to subtract an hour from what your watch says and look under 12:00 PM. Where the column "Beginning of July" and the horizontal line "11–12 PM" intersect, you find 8; therefore map N II/August on page 44 applies. Or: You are in North Dakota and want to find out where you will find Orion on December 28, at about 4:30 A.M. December 28 can be considered the beginning of January, and at the intersection of the appropriate row and column you find—nothing. The missing section of the sky lies *between* the maps for May and April, and we therefore turn to map N I/May on page 33 and, if we are interested in a star close to the horizon, we may also want to look at map N I/April. Don't worry about the fact that the maps you are using are labeled August (in the first example) and May (in the second) even though you are watching the sky in July and in December. The indicated months apply only for the usual stargazing time of 8 to 10 PM. (or, during daylight saving time, 9 to 11 PM).

When and Where Can One See the Planets?

The planets and the moon do not appear in the star maps because they move across the sky so quickly that their course would have to be entered anew every year. When looking for planets, what we have to go on is that they (and the moon) always are to be found only on the ecliptic, which is marked on every map. And since only the zodiacal constellations are located on the ecliptic (see page 11), those are the only constellation names you will find in notes referring to the planets. These notes mention which planets can be seen where in the evening (until about midnight) and, in parentheses, in the morning (after midnight). In the maps of series N I and N II all the indicated times from April through October have already been translated into daylight saving time.

Let us look at a couple of examples: In 1993 the planet Saturn becomes visible in June between the parallels of 40 and 60 degrees north latitude (map series N I) in the constellation Capricorn at 1 AM (see page 22). In June, daylight saving time is in effect. We therefore have to subtract an hour before consulting the table on the inside back cover. Now, if we read across from "11 PM to 12 PM" to the column for June, we find that map N I/July (page 23) applies. On this map the ecliptic runs through the constellations Scorpius, Sagittarius, and Capricorn to the southeastern horizon. Saturn consequently must appear there, on the ecliptic, in the constellation Capricorn, at 1 AM daylight saving time. At the end of June and in early July, map N I/August already applies, and on this map Capricorn and consequently the ecliptic are already quite a bit higher in the southern sky, so that Saturn can be more easily watched at the end of the month. The following general rules will help you recognize which shining points in the sky are which planets:

- Generally, all planets appear very bright and can be mistaken only for the very brightest stars. The light of planets does not flicker but appears clear and steady.
- Mercury is the most difficult planet to observe. It always shows up for a maximum of only one hour—low in the western sky right after sunset and in the east before sunrise.
- Venus, too, can be seen only after sunset in the west, when it appears as the "evening star," or else before sunrise in the east as the "morning star." It is the most luminous of all the celestial bodies (except for the moon and the sun).
- Mars is easy to recognize by its red color (more a reddish tint than a true red). Because of its color it is often referred to as the "red planet."
- Jupiter always appears very bright (usually brighter than Mars and Saturn but fainter than Venus) and shines with an unmistakable yellowish light.
- Saturn's light, finally, is a neutral white. This planet will remain near the stars of the constellation Aquarius through 1995.

Table of the Lunar Phases

Year	Jan	Feb	Mar	Apr	May	Jun	Jul	Aug	Sep	Oct	Nov	Dec
1992	4, 12, 19, 26	3, 11, 18, 25	4, 11, 18, 25	2, 10, 16, 24	2, 9, 16, 24, 31	7, **14**, 23, 30	6, 14, 22, 29	5, 13, 21, 27	3, 11, 19, 26	3, 11, 18, 25	2, 10, 17, 24	2, **9**, 16, **23**, 31
1993	8, 14, 22, 30	6, 13, 21	1, 8, 14, 23, 30	6, 13, 21, 29	5, 13, 21, 28	**4**, 12, 19, 26	3, 11, 19, 25	2, 10, 17, 24, 31	9, 15, 22, 30	8, 15, 22, 30	7, **13**, 20, **29**	6, 13, 20, 28
1994	4, 11, 19, 27	3, 10, 18, 25	4, 12, 20, 27	2, 10, 18, 25	2, **10**, 18, **24**, 31	9, 16, 23, 30	8, 15, 22, 30	7, 14, 21, 29	5, 12, 19, 24	4, 11, 19, 27	**3**, 10, 18, 26	2, 9, 17, 25
1995	1, 8, 16, 23, 30	7, 15, 22	1, 9, 16, 23, 30	8, **15**, 21, **29**	7, 14, 21, 29	6, 12, 19, 27	5, 12, 19, 27	3, 10, 17, 25	2, 8, 16, 24	1, 8, 16, **24**, 30	7, 15, 22, 29	6, 15, 21, 28

● = New moon;   ◐ = First quarter;   ○ = Full moon;   ◑ = Last quarter

A number in boldface type with ● = Solar eclipse; with ○ = Lunar eclipse

Star Map Series N I

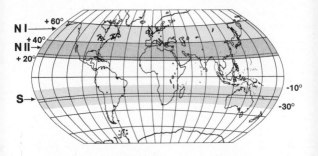

Star Maps and Constellations

The maps in Series N I are for the latitudes between 40 and 60 degrees north. Applicable for the northern United States, Canada, northern, central, and eastern Europe, that is, the Benelux countries, Scandinavia, Germany, Austria, Switzerland, northern Italy, France, Great Britain, Poland, Czechoslovakia, Hungary, Romania, Yugoslavia, Bulgaria, and Russia.

Reminders:

If you travel to areas farther south, turn to the map series N II (see page 41). Should you want to identify stars north of 60 degrees north latitude, you will notice that the stars in the south are lower and those in the north higher in the sky. The positions of the stars and constellations in relation to each other remain unchanged.

From April through October, daylight saving time is adopted in many countries. The positions of the planets are therefore given in terms of daylight saving time for these months.

In regions north of 60 degrees north latitude, the nights are not dark enough during the summer for observing stars. This is the period of twilight nights and, north of the arctic circle (at 66–50°), the period of the midnight sun. There, the sun stays in the sky 24 hours a day at this time of year.

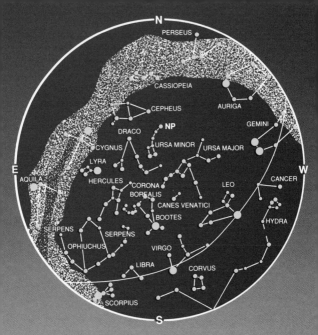

Celestial Events during June

Summer officially begins on June 20 at 11:14 PM in 1992, on June 21 at 5 AM in 1993, and on June 21 at 10:48 AM in 1994. (Winter begins on the same date in the southern hemisphere.)

1992: Jupiter is in Leo and visible for about an hour after sunset. (Saturn is visible in Capricorn from 2 AM on. Mars is in the morning sky from 3 AM on in the constellations Pisces and Aries.)

1993: Mars is in the western part of Leo, and Jupiter just to the east in Virgo. Their apparent distance from each other continues to shrink and they are joined by Mercury in the evening sky. On June 4, a total lunar eclipse is visible from eastern Asia and Australia. (Saturn, in Capricorn, rises about 1 AM.)

1994: Early in June, Mercury is in one of its best viewing positions, in Gemini and Taurus. Venus glows ever brighter during the month, setting about three hours after the sun. Jupiter dominates the rest of the evenings in Virgo. (Saturn, in Aquarius, is visible from about 1 AM on.)

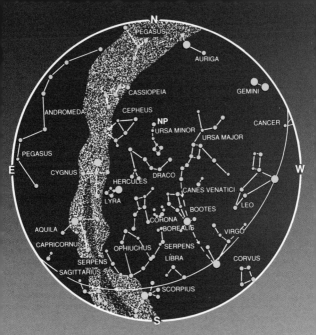

Celestial Events during July

The distance between Earth and the sun is at its annual maximum, 94.3 million miles (152.1 million km). This occurs on July 3 at 8 AM in 1992, on July 4 at 6 PM in 1993, and on July 5, at 3 PM in 1994. Note another use for the Big Dipper: Use an arc from the handle to find Arcturus in Boötes, then continue the arc down to Spica, the only bright star that makes Virgo obvious.

1992: Jupiter is in Leo; Saturn, in Capricorn. (Mars is in Aries and Taurus in the eastern sky from 1 AM on.)

1993: Jupiter, in Virgo, and Mars, in Leo, both set before midnight. Although it is much farther away, by this time Jupiter's yellowish light has become noticeably brighter than Mars. (Saturn, in Capricorn, is visible from 11 PM on.)

1994: Venus moves out of Leo to join Jupiter in Virgo by the end of July. Venus is now by far the brightest point of light in the sky. (Saturn, in Aquarius, can be seen through the latter part of the night, rising at about 11 PM. Mars, in Taurus, is visible from 2 AM on.)

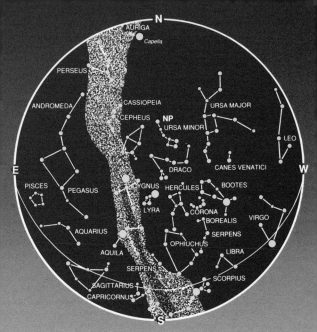

Celestial Events during August

Between August 8 and 13, large numbers of meteors emanate from Perseus. Normally, six or seven meteors can be seen each hour in a dark sky. At maximum, the Perseid shower provides about 50 per hour. Best viewing is around 2 AM.

1992: On August 7, Saturn is in its best viewing position of the year in Capricorn. Early in the month, Jupiter and Venus move ever closer together until lost in the twilight glow by the 15th. (Mars, in Taurus, can be seen from 1 AM on in the eastern sky.)

1993: Saturn appears in the evening sky for the first time this year; on the 14th, it is at opposition, which means it rises at sunset in Capricorn. Jupiter and Mars appear to move closer together during the month, in Virgo.

1994: Venus is at its greatest brightness for this year, but Jupiter, to the south almost matches Venus' brightness this month. Both are in Virgo. Saturn rises in Aquarius just after sunset. (Mars, in Gemini, rises about 1 AM.)

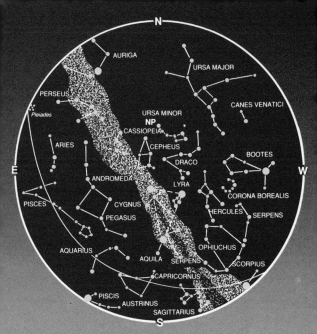

Celestial Events during September

Autumn officially starts on September 22 at 2:43 PM in 1992, on the 22nd at 8:22 PM in 1993, and on the 23rd at 2:19 AM in 1994. Days and nights are about equal, now, but soon the nights will be getting longer, especially in the high northern latitudes. The brilliant Summer Triangle is almost straight overhead early September evenings.

1992: Venus shines as the evening star in the west until about 7:30 PM. Saturn is in Capricorn. (Mars is in Gemini in the eastern sky after 11 PM.)

1993: Mars and Jupiter are in close conjunction on September 7. They appear only briefly, in Virgo. Saturn remains the planet of the first half of the night. (Venus, in Leo, is now well placed as the "morning star.")

1994: Jupiter and Venus seem to be moving closer together in Libra, but without coming as close together as Mars and Jupiter did last year. Both are visible only briefly after sunset in the north. Saturn appears in Aquarius in the evening sky on September 1.

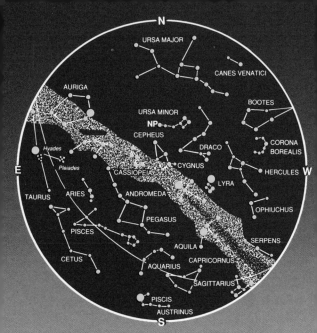

Celestial Events during October

Starting this month, daylight saving time is no longer in effect in western Europe, but it continues in the United States in most areas until the last Sunday in October. The clocks are then set back one hour effective at 2 AM on October 25 in 1992, on the 31st in 1993, and on the 30th in 1995.

1992: Saturn is in Capricorn; Venus appears for about an hour, until 7 PM, low in the western sky; Mars is in the east in the constellation Gemini from 11 PM on. (The careful observer may catch a glimpse of Jupiter in the morning twilight. It is near the Leo-Virgo border this month.)

1993: Saturn is the only visible planet, appearing in Capricorn, at sunset.

1994: On October 7, Jupiter will appear very close to the moon for northern hemisphere observers. Mercury disappears from the sky during the first week of October, as does Venus in the middle of the month, leaving only Saturn, in Aquarius, to be observed in the evening sky. (Mars, now in Cancer, is visible after 1 AM—midnight once standard time goes back into effect.)

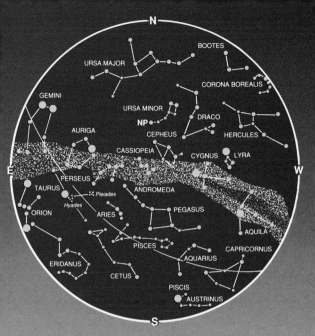

Celestial Events during November

1992: Saturn is in Capricorn, visible most of the night. Mars is in Gemini and rises about 8 PM. Venus, in Sagittarius, is in the western sky until about 7 PM. (Jupiter is in the morning sky from 5 AM on in Virgo.)

1993: This year, November brings several celestial events. First on the 6th, a rare transit of Mercury will occur. The tiny planet passes in front of the sun as seen from earth. On the 29th, observers in North and South America, western Europe, and northeastern Asia can see a total lunar eclipse. (Although Jupiter begins to appear in the morning sky near the end of the month and Mars may be glimpsed in the evening twilight at the beginning of November, Saturn is the only visible planet this month.)

1994: For southern observers, a solar eclipse can be seen. Saturn, in Aquarius, is the only planet visible in the evening sky. (Mars, in Leo, rises about 11 PM and can be seen through the rest of the night. Venus begins to appear in the morning twilight near the end of the month.)

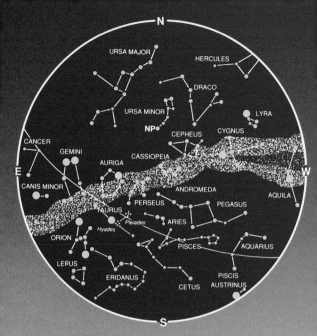

Celestial Events during December

Winter officially begins on December 21 at 9:43 AM in 1992, on the 21st at 3:26 PM in 1993, and on the 21st, at 9:23 PM in 1994.

1992: On December 9, there is a total lunar eclipse over Europe fully visible at midnight in Germany, Austria, and Switzerland. On the 24th, a partial solar eclipse can be seen over the north Pacific. Saturn and Venus appear very close together on the 21st in Capricorn, visible in the western sky until 9 PM; Mars is in Gemini (Jupiter is in Virgo from 3 AM on.)

1993: This year comes to a close with only Saturn easily visible in the evening sky. It is in the border area between Capricorn and Aquarius, but leaves the sky about 10 pm. (Jupiter is the only other planet visible this month. It rises in Virgo at about 4 AM.)

1994: Saturn, in Aquarius, is the only easily visible planet at sunset, but at 9:30 PM, Mars rises in Leo. (Venus is in Libra and rises after 4 AM, followed by Jupiter, in Scorpius, at about 5:30 AM.)

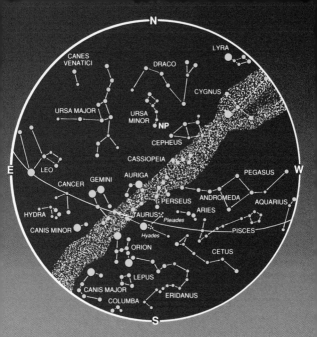

Celestial Events during January

The distance between Earth and the sun is at its annual minimum: only 91.2 million miles (147.1 million km). This occurs on January 3 at 10 PM in 1993; on January 2 at 1 AM in 1994; and on January 4 at 6 AM in 1995.

1993: Venus is the "evening star," appearing in the west for a few hours in Aquarius. Mars is up most of the night in the constellation Gemini. (Jupiter rises about 1 AM in Virgo.)

1994: Saturn can be seen in the west after sunset all month, setting a few hours later. By the end of the month, Mercury joins Saturn very low in the evening sky, so Saturn can be used as a guide to finding this elusive planet. (Jupiter, in Libra, rises after 2 AM.)

1995: Mercury and Saturn are again visible in the evening sky. Saturn can be seen the entire month in Aquarius. One may catch a glimpse of Mercury in Capricorn around the 15th. Mars rises in the late evening. (Jupiter and Venus rise in Scorpius about two hours before the sun.)

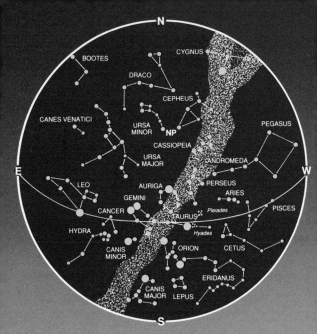

Celestial Events during February

Look for the "Winter Hexagon"—the stars Castor and Pollux, in Gemini, Capella in Auriga, Aldeberan in Taurus, Rigel in Orion, and Sirius in Canis Major. Along with Betelgeuse, these stars give an opportunity to see most of the brightest stars all at the same time. They are well placed, almost directly overhead on February evenings.

1993: Mars, in Gemini, and Venus, in Pisces, dominate the early evening sky, but Venus is very low by the end of the month. Jupiter rises before midnight in Virgo.

1994: Mercury and Saturn start the month low in the western sky at sunset, but quickly disappear in the evening twilight. (Jupiter is now in Libra and can be seen after midnight.)

1995: While Saturn quickly disappears from the evening sky, Mars returns. It is directly opposite the sun on February 12 and on that date rises at sunset. (Jupiter rises in Scorpius after 3 AM.)

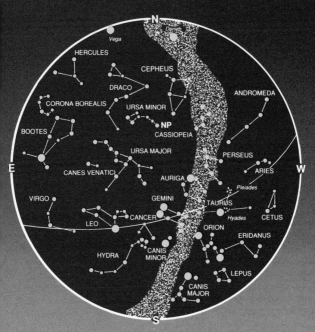

Celestial Events during March

Spring officially begins on March 20 at 9:41 AM in 1993, on the 20th at 3:28 PM in 1994, and on the 20th at 9:14 PM in 1995. This means nearly equal periods of day and night, warmer temperatures, and nevertheless some of the best bright star groupings of the winter sky. The Big Dipper is now well placed overhead to help find directions in the sky.

1993: Mars, still in Gemini, is the only planet easily visible at sunset. Jupiter appears in Virgo at about 9 PM at the beginning of the month and rises earlier and earlier each night.

1994: No planets are visible in the early evening. (By the time Jupiter rises in Libra, it is already past 11 PM.)

1995: Mars is quite bright this month in the constellations Cancer and Leo. (Jupiter rises in Scorpius at about 3 AM.)

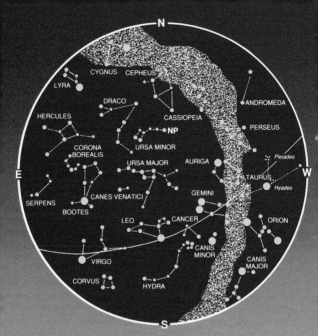

Celestial Events during April

During April, daylight saving time goes into effect. While dates and times vary, the standard in most areas of the United States is to set the clocks ahead one hour effective at 2 AM on the first Sunday of this month. This means, where used, daylight saving time begins on April 4, 1993, on April 3, 1994, and on April 2, 1995.

1993: Jupiter and Mars dominate the evening sky. Mars is the farthest west, in Gemini. Jupiter is in Virgo. (Saturn rises just before sunrise in Aquarius.)

1994: Venus appears as the "evening star." The 12th to the 13th, the moon passes in front of Venus as seen from the Arctic. From other areas the moon appears very close to Venus. Jupiter can be seen in Libra after 10 PM.

1995: A partial eclipse of the moon occurs on the night of the 15th, and an annular solar eclipse on the 29th, but neither is visible from this latitude. One must travel to Central or South America to see these eclipses. Planets visible this month are Mars in Cancer (Jupiter, in Scorpius, in the morning sky).

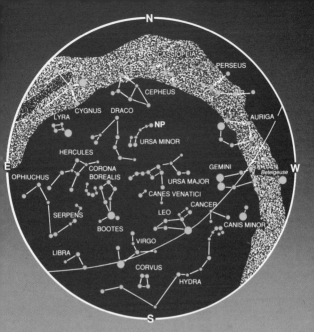

Celestial Events during May

1993: Mars, in Cancer, and Jupiter, in Virgo, continue in the evening sky. Both are well placed for early evening viewing. A partial solar eclipse on the 21st is visible in North America and northern Europe. (Saturn is moving into the morning sky now, rising about one hour before the sun.)

1994: Venus grows brighter and higher in the evening sky. By the time it sets, Jupiter is high enough to be easily observed in Libra. On May 10, an annular solar eclipse can be seen in most of North, Central, and South America. Maximum eclipse can be seen in New England and eastern Canada.

1995: Mars, in Leo, is in the evening sky all month and is joined briefly by tiny Mercury. In the middle of the month, the planet innermost to the sun can be seen by the careful northern hemisphere observer in the northwestern sky just after sunset. (Jupiter becomes visible about 10 PM, in Scorpius. Saturn, in Aquarius, rises about 4 AM. On the 22nd, the rings of Saturn are edge-on as seen from earth, so even in larger telescopes, they are not visible.)

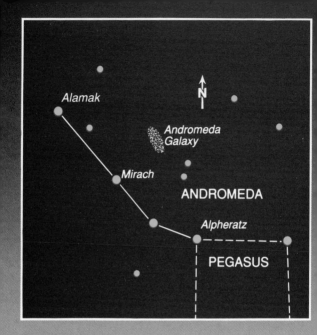

Andromeda

In any discussion of Andromeda, the most famous object in the constellation is bound to be mentioned, namely, the Andromeda Galaxy. Its technical name is M 31. (M stands for Charles Messier, an eighteenth-century French astronomer who compiled a consecutively numbered catalog of celestial objects that appeared nebulous—hence M 31.) The Andromeda Galaxy is the third closest major galaxy after the two Magellanic Clouds (see color photo on page 13). M 31 is composed of over 400 billion stars that are arranged in a huge spiral. The Andromeda Galaxy is 2.7 million light-years away from Earth. We highly recommend that you observe it through binoculars on some clear night.

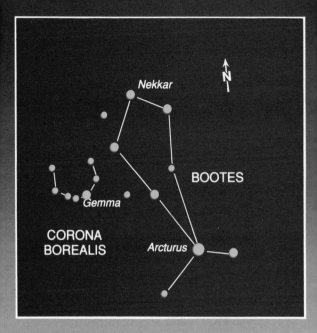

Boötes (the Herdsman) and Corona Borealis (the Northern Crown)

The constellation Boötes contains the brightest star of the northern celestial hemisphere, namely, Arcturus, which stands out because of its reddish color. A tip on how to find Arcturus easily is given in connection with the star map N1/July (see page 23). Every light ray from Arcturus that reaches us here on Earth has traveled through space for 36 years. Astronomers express this by saying the star is 36 light-years away; this is equivalent to 211 trillion miles (340 trillion km)!

The Northern Crown has a counterpart in the southern celestial hemisphere (see page 79). But the Northern Crown includes an exceptionally brilliant jewel, the star Gemma (Latin for "jewel"). The Southern Crown (Corona Australis) has nothing comparable to offer. Gemma is 71 light-years away from Earth.

Ursa Major (the Great Bear) and Canes Venatici (the Hunting Dogs)

Ursa Major is among the best known constellations of the northern sky. Its seven brightest stars—all with sonorous names—make up the Big Dipper, which is not, however, an officially recognized constellation by itself. Make sure to have a good look at the star Mizar; it is often said to be a good test of one's eyesight. Right next to Mizar you may be able, if your eyes are good, to spot Alcor, which means "little charioteer." In Europe the Big Dipper is often referred to as the "Big Wagon," and Alcor, the "little charioteer," is said to ride on the horses that are harnessed to the wagon shaft (the handle of the Big Dipper).

For all practical purposes Canes Venatici has only one bright star, Cor Caroli, which means "heart of Charles." Edmund Halley, the astronomer, named this star in 1725 in honor of King Charles II of England.

Ursa Minor (the Little Bear) and Draco (the Dragon)

The most famous star in Ursa Minor is Polaris, the north star. It marks the north celestial pole like a beacon, though, as the map shows, it is not positioned exactly on the pole. But its being off the mark by one degree is of no great consequence to the stargazer. Once you spot Polaris in the sky you know where north is. The constellation Draco is not nearly as prominent. But if you have a pair of binoculars you will be able to tell quite clearly that the star Nu Draconis is a double star, or binary. Nu Draconis consists of two stars that lie close to each other, revolve around each other, and look to the naked eye like a single star.

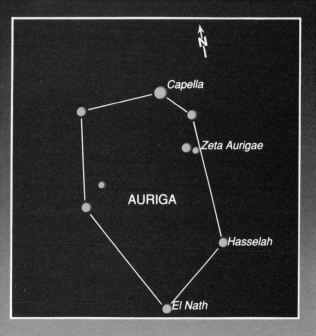

Auriga (the Charioteer)

The most interesting star in Auriga is not the one that shines most brightly, Capella, but Zeta Aurigae. It may sound incredible, but Zeta Aurigae can be "X-rayed," and this is how we know that it consists of two separate stars. One of them is 293 times larger than the sun; the other is only five times the sun's size. The two stars revolve around each other, and because the smaller is so tiny in comparison to its larger brother it acts like an X-ray lamp when it disappears behind the bigger star every $2\frac{1}{2}$ years. An examination of the light rays has given us some highly interesting information on the structure of the giant star. The star El Nath, though included in the figure of Auriga, is actually part of the constellation Taurus.

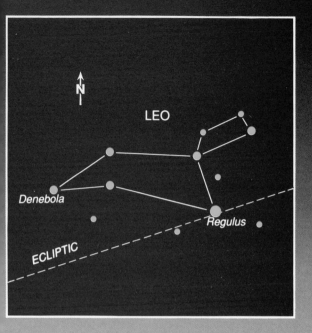

Leo (the Lion)

The constellation Leo is particularly easy to locate in the sky. Its stars form two trapezoids that can readily be imagined to represent a lion. According to Greek myth this lion was of monstrous strength and could be slain only by Hercules. The star Regulus ("little king") counts among the twenty brightest stars of the sky and is four times bigger than the sun. It is 68 light-years away from Earth. Together with Spica (see page 56) and Antares (see page 79) it is among the brightest stars that lie exactly on the ecliptic. That is why planets are often seen near these stars (see pages 18–19).

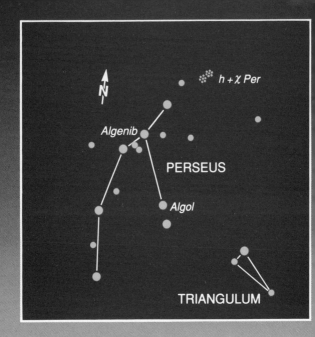

Perseus

Algol, the "demon star," is one of the most interesting stars in the sky. Although it looks like a single star not only to the naked eye but also through a telescope, it in fact consists of two stars that revolve around each other, mutually eclipsing each other every 2 1/2 days. When one star is in front of the other their combined brightness decreases, of course, and Algol is therefore called an "eclipsing" variable. The fluctuations in brightness can be noticed even by the unaided eye.

The double star cluster h and chi Persei should really be observed through binoculars. Both clusters, which are 8,000 light-years away from us, are quite spectacular. (Star clusters are aggregations of a few hundred to several thousand stars.)

Star Map Series N II

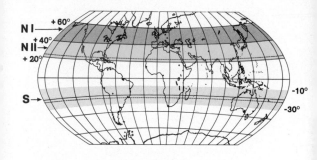

Star Maps and Constellations

The maps in Series N II are for the latitudes between 20 and 40 degrees north. Applicable in the United States, Mexico, the Caribbean, southern Europe, including Spain, Portugal, southern Italy, and Greece; also for Turkey, Lebanon, Israel, Egypt, Tunisia, Algeria, Morocco, Persia, Pakistan, Afghanistan, India, Thailand, Burma, China, Korea, Japan, and Taiwan.

Reminders:

In these latitudes constellations of the southern celestial hemisphere first become visible, such as the famous Southern Cross (see N II/May, page 53). The closer you are to the equator, the more clearly you will be able to see these constellations in the southern sky. From April through October, daylight saving time (DST) is in effect in many countries. Therefore, the positions of the planets are given in daylight saving time for this period. The closer you are to the equator, the faster darkness will fall in the evening and the earlier you will be able to detect the stars and the planets. Dusk is much briefer in the tropics than in regions farther north or south of the equator. The sun as well as all the other heavenly bodies rise and set more vertically and therefore rise and set more quickly.

41

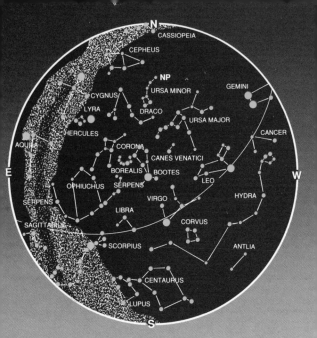

Celestial Events during June

Summer officially begins on June 20 at 11:14 PM in 1992, on the 21st at 5 AM in 1993, and on the 21st at 10:48 AM in 1994.

1992: Jupiter is in Leo and visible for about an hour after sunset. A partial lunar eclipse is visible on the 15th from Mexico, the Caribbean, and south Atlantic. (Saturn is visible in Capricorn from 2 AM on. Mars in is the morning sky from 3 AM on in the constellations Pisces and Aries.)

1993: Mars is in the western part of Leo, and Jupiter just to the east in Virgo. Their apparent distance from each other continues to shrink and they are joined by Mercury in the evening sky. On June 4 there is a total lunar eclipse visible from eastern Asia and Australia. (Saturn, in Capricorn, rises about 1 AM.)

1994: Early in June, Mercury is in one of its best viewing positions, in Gemini and Taurus, best visible in the northern hemisphere. Venus glows ever brighter during the month, setting about three hours after the sun. Jupiter dominates the rest of the evening in Virgo. (Saturn, in Aquarius, is visible from about 1 AM on.)

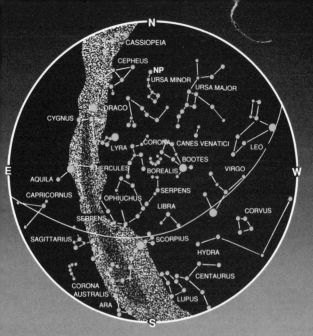

Celestial Events during July

The distance between Earth and the sun is at its annual maximum: 94.3 million miles (152.1 million km). For dates and times, see page 23. The summer Milky Way is at its best during July and August. Look with binoculars, especially in the region surrounding Scorpius and Sagittarius (toward the center of our galaxy). This area is richly dotted with star clusters and nebulae.

1992: Jupiter is in Leo; Saturn, in Capricorn. (Mars is in Aries and Taurus in the eastern sky from 1 AM on.)

1993: Jupiter, in Virgo, and Mars, in Leo, both set before midnight. Although it is much farther away by this time, Jupiter's yellowish light has become noticeably brighter than Mars'. (Saturn, in Capricorn, is visible from 11 PM on.)

1994: Venus moves out of Leo to join Jupiter in Virgo by the end of the month. Venus is now by far the brightest point of light in the sky. (Saturn, in Aquarius, can be seen through the latter part of the night, rising at about 11 PM. Mars, in Taurus, is visible from 2 AM on.)

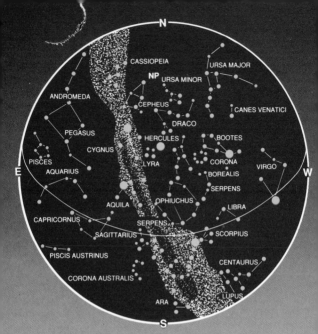

Celestial Events during August

Between August 8 and 13, large numbers of shooting stars, or meteors, emanate from Perseus. Not quite as high in the sky as in more northern latitudes, this shower is still well worth watching for. About 50 meteors should appear per hour at the peak, usually about 2 AM on the 11th or 12th.

1992: On August 7, Saturn is in its best viewing position of the year in Capricorn. Early in the month, Jupiter and Venus move ever closer together until lost in the twilight glow by the 15th. (Mars, in Taurus, can be seen from 1 AM on in the eastern sky.)

1993: Saturn appears in the evening sky for the first time this year; on the 14th, it is at opposition, which means it rises at sunset in Capricorn. Jupiter and Mars appear to move closer together during the month, in Virgo.

1994: Venus is at its greatest brightness for this year, but Jupiter, to the south, almost matches Venus' brightness this month. Both are in Virgo. Saturn rises in Aquarius just after sunset. (Mars, in Gemini, rises about 1 AM.)

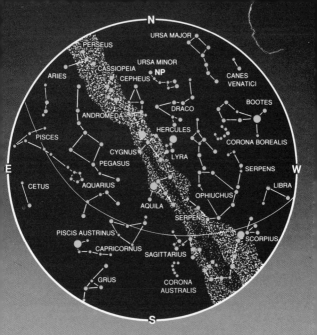

Celestial Events during September

Autumn officially starts September 22 at 2:43 PM in 1992, on the 22nd at 8:22 PM in 1993, and on the 23rd at 2:19 AM in 1994. The star Fomalhaut in Piscis Austrinus is really the only bright star associated with the fall sky, but see if you can make out the Great Square of Pegasus directly between Pisces and Cygnus.

1992: Venus shines as the evening star in the west until about 7:30 PM. Saturn is in Capricorn. (Mars is in Gemini in the eastern sky after 11 PM.)

1993: Mars and Jupiter are in close conjunction on the 7th. They appear in the evening sky, only briefly, in Virgo. Saturn remains the planet of the first half of the night. (Venus, in Leo, is now well placed as the "morning star.")

1994: Jupiter and Venus seem to be moving closer together in Libra, but without coming as close together as Mars and Jupiter did last year. Both are visible only briefly after sunset in the north. Saturn appears in Aquarius in the evening sky on the 1st.

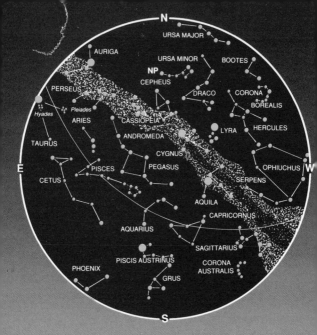

Celestial Events during October

Starting this month, daylight saving time is no longer in effect in western Europe, but it continues in the United States in most areas until the last Sunday in October. For dates see page 26.

1992: Saturn is in Capricorn; Venus appears for about an hour, until 7 PM, low in the western sky; Mars is in the east in the constellation Gemini from 11 pm on. The moon passes in front of Mercury as seen from the Caribbean, North Africa, Italy, and Greece on October 27. The next night, the moon covers Venus as seen from North Africa and Arabia. In the western hemisphere, the 1st should make for a good opportunity to find elusive Mercury.

1993: Saturn is the only visible planet, appearing in Capricorn, at sunset.

1994: On the night of October 7, Jupiter will appear very close to the moon. Mercury disappears from the sky during the first week of October, as does Venus in the middle of the month, leaving only Saturn, in Aquarius. (Mars, now in Cancer, is visible after 1 AM—midnight standard time.

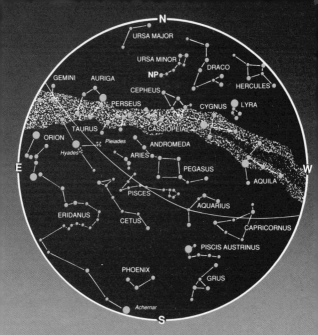

Celestial Events during November

1992: Saturn is in Capricorn, visible most of the night. Mars is in Gemini and rises about 8 PM. Venus is in Sagittarius in the western sky until about 7 PM. (Jupiter is in the morning sky from 5 AM on in Virgo.)

1993: This year, November brings several celestial events. On the 6th, a rare transit of Mercury will occur. The tiny planet passes in front of the sun as seen from earth. On the 29th, observers in North and South America, western Europe, and northeastern Asia can see a total lunar eclipse. (Although Jupiter begins to appear in the morning sky near the end of the month, and Mars may be glimpsed in the evening twilight at the beginning of November, Saturn is the only easily visible planet this month.)

1994: For southern observers, a solar eclipse can be seen. Saturn, in Aquarius, is the only planet visible in the evening sky. (Mars, in Leo, rises about 11 pm and can be seen through the rest of the night. Venus begins to appear in the morning twilight near the end of the month.

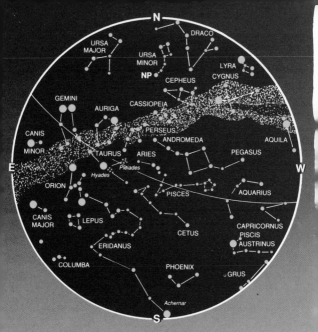

Celestial Events during December

Winter officially begins on December 21 at 9:43 AM in 1992, on the 21st at 3:26 PM in 1993, and on the 21st at 9:23 PM in 1994.

1992: On the 9th, there is a total lunar eclipse over Europe fully visible at midnight in Germany, Austria, and Switzerland. On the 24th, a partial solar eclipse can be seen over the north Pacific. Saturn and Venus appear very close together on the 21st in Capricorn, visible in the western sky until 9 PM; Mars is in Gemini. (Jupiter is in Virgo from 3 AM on.)

1993: This year comes to a close with only Saturn easily visible in the evening sky. It is in the border area between Capricorn and Aquarius, but leaves the sky about 10 PM. (Jupiter is the only other planet visible this month. It rises in Virgo at about 4 AM.)

1994: Saturn, in Aquarius, is the only easily visible planet at sunset, but at 9:30 PM, Mars rises in Leo. (Venus is in Libra and rises after 4 AM, followed by Jupiter, in Scorpius, at about 5:30.)

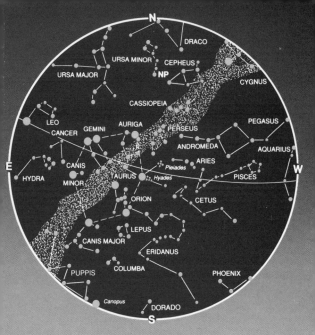

Celestial Events during January

Earth reaches its shortest distance to the sun, only 91.2 million miles (147.1 million km) in January. For dates and times see page 29. Look for the "Winter Hexagon," made up of Castor and Pollux, in Gemini. Capella in Auriga, Aldebaran in Taurus, Rigel in Orion, and Sirius in Canis Major.

1993: Venus is the "evening star," appearing in the west for a few hours in Aquarius. Mars is up most of the night in the constellation Gemini. (Jupiter rises about 1 AM in Virgo.)

1994: Saturn can be seen all month in the west after sunset setting a few hours later. By the end of the month, Mercury joins Saturn very low in the evening sky. (Jupiter, in Libra, rises after 2 AM.)

1995: Mercury and Saturn are again visible in the evening sky. Saturn can be seen the entire month in Aquarius. One may catch a glimpse of Mercury in Capricorn around the 15th. Mars rises in the late evening. (Jupiter and Venus rise about two hours before the sun in Scorpius.)

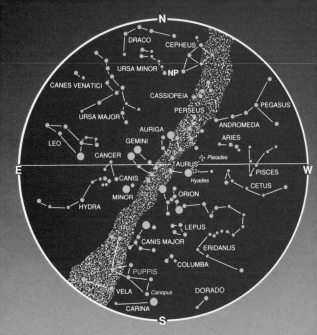

Celestial Events during February

In February from this latitude, the ecliptic cuts across the sky from due east to due west, which means the planets will be found along an east-west meridian in the early evening. The cooler air this time of year creates some of the best viewing conditions available. Bright Canopus makes a rare early evening appearance just above the southern horizon from lower northern latitudes.

1993: Mars, in Gemini, and Venus, in Pisces, dominate the early evening sky, but Venus is very low by the end of the month. Jupiter rises before midnight in Virgo.

1994: Mercury and Saturn start the month low in the western sky at sunset, but quickly disappear in the evening twilight. (Jupiter is now in Libra and can be seen after midnight.)

1995: While Saturn quickly disappears from the evening sky, Mars returns. It is directly opposite the sun on February 12 and on that date rises at sunset. (Jupiter rises after 3 AM in Scorpius.)

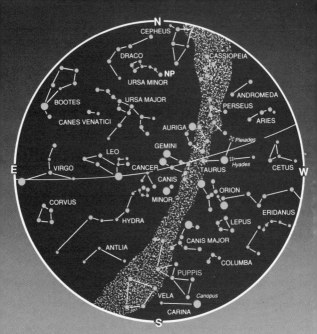

Celestial Events during March

Spring officially begins on March 20 at 9:41 AM in 1993, on the 20th at 3:28 PM in 1994, and the 20th at 9:14 PM in 1995. This means the sun will be getting higher in the sky. The days will get longer and the nights shorter. Now that the Big Dipper is a little higher in the early evening, it can be used easily to find Polaris, the North Star (marked by "NP" on the map). The three brightest stars of the spring sky, Regulus in Leo, Spica in Virgo, and Arcturus in Boötes can also be seen in the eastern sky.

1993: Mars, still in Gemini, is the only planet easily visible at sunset. Jupiter appears at about 9 PM in Virgo at the beginning of the month and rises earlier and earlier each night.

1994: No planets are visible in the early evening. (By the time Jupiter rises in Libra, it is already past 11 PM.)

1995: Mars, now in the constellations Cancer and Leo, is quite bright this month. (Jupiter rises at about 3 AM in Scorpius.)

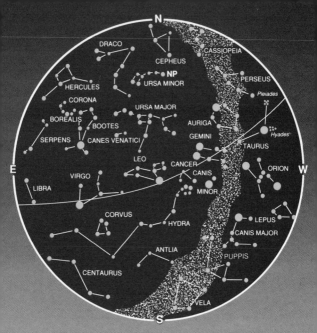

Celestial Events during April

During April, daylight saving time goes into effect. While dates and times vary, the standard in most areas of the United States is to set the clocks ahead one hour effective at 2 AM on the first Sunday of April. For exact dates, see page 32.

1993: Jupiter and Mars dominate the evening sky. Mars is the farther west, in Gemini. Jupiter is in Virgo. (Saturn rises before sunrise in Aquarius.)

1994: Venus begins to appear as the "evening star." The night of the 12th to the 13th, the moon passes in front of Venus as seen from the high Arctic latitudes. From other areas it will appear very close to Venus. Jupiter is well placed after 10 PM and can be seen the rest of the night in Libra.

1995: A partial eclipse of the moon is visible on the night of April 15, and an annular solar eclipse on the 29th, but neither is visible from this latitude. One must travel to Central or South America to see these eclipses. Planets visible this month are Mars in Cancer (Jupiter, in Scorpius, in the morning sky.)

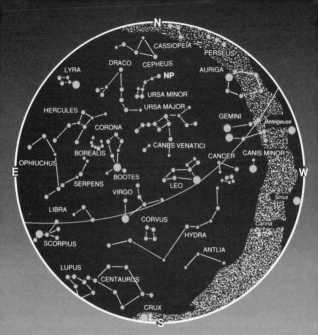

Celestial Events during May

1993: Mars, in Cancer, and Jupiter, in Virgo, continue in the evening sky. Both are well placed for early evening viewing. A partial solar eclipse on May 21 is visible in North America and northern Europe. (Saturn is moving into the morning sky now, rising about one hour before the sun.)

1994: Venus grows brighter and higher in the evening sky. By the time it sets, Jupiter is high enough in the sky to be easily observed in Libra. On May 10, an annular solar eclipse can be seen throughout most of North, Central, and South America. Maximum eclipse can be seen at high northern latitudes.

1995: Mars, in Leo, is in the evening sky all month and is joined briefly by tiny Mercury. In the middle of the month the careful northern hemisphere observer can see the planet innermost to the sun in the northwestern sky just after sunset. (Jupiter, in Scorpius, becomes visible about 10 pm. Saturn, in Aquarius, rises about 4 AM. On May 22, the rings of Saturn are edge-on as seen from earth, so even in larger telescopes, they are not visible.)

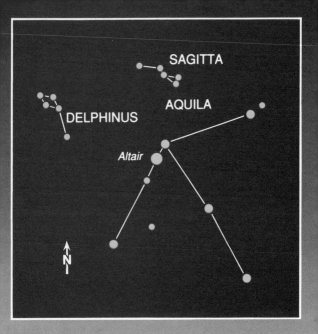

Aquila (the Eagle)

Of the constellations that do not appear in the round star maps, some of the most important ones will be individually presented here. Aquila is bordered by Delphinus (the Dolphin) on the northeast and by Sagitta (the Arrow) on the north. The four stars arranged in a diamond shape are the most striking feature of Delphinus. Sagitta is said to represent the arrow with which Hercules killed the gods' eagle. The star Altair in Aquila—along with Vega in Lyra and Deneb in Cygnus (see page 59)—is one of the brightest stars in the northern summer sky (see map NI/September on page 25). It is 16 light-years away (that amounts to 94 trillion miles or 151 trillion km) and thus one of our solar system's close neighbors.

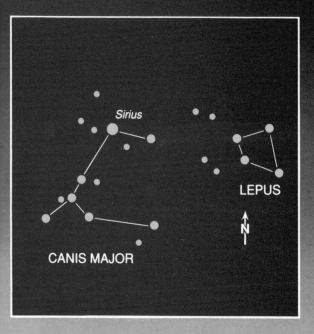

Canis Major (the Great Dog) and Lepus (the Hare)

By far the most conspicuous part of Canis Major is Sirius, the brightest star in the sky (only some of the planets outshine it). There are stars that generate a lot more light than Sirius does, but Sirius is fairly close to us; a "mere" 8.6 light-years or 53 trillion miles (86 trillion km) separate us from it. Because of this proximity a relatively large amount of light reaches Earth from this star, just as a light bulb directly overhead appears brighter to us than the much more powerful beam of a lighthouse that is far away. The apparent brightness of stars thus tells us something not only about their light output but also about their distance.

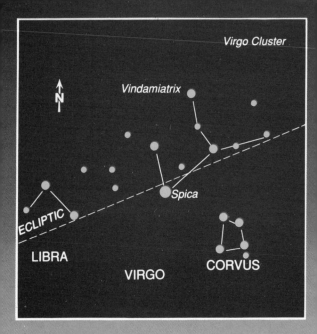

Virgo (the Maiden), Corvus (the Crow or Raven), Libra (the Scales)

Of these constellations, only Virgo contains components of special interest. There is first of all the star Spica, which according to Greek myth is the ear of wheat the maiden (daughter of Ceres) held in her hand. Spica (distance from Earth: 218 light-years) can be located just like Arcturus (in Boötes) by extending the curve of the Big Dipper's handle (see N I/July on page 23). Another reason for Virgo's fame is the so-called Virgo Cluster. Here 22 percent of all the known galaxies of the northern celestial hemisphere are crowded together in a very small area. This is a truly amazing concentration of galaxies, most of which can, however, be seen only through very large telescopes. Galaxies are huge disk-shaped formations of stars, gases and dust that are many millions of light-years away from us.

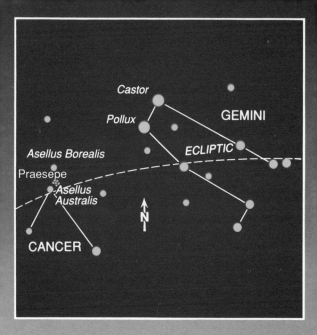

Cancer (the Crab) and Gemini (the Twins)

Praesepe, or the Beehive, is one of the best known open star clusters. At a distance of 550 light-years, about 500 stars are gathered there and present an impressive sight when viewed through binoculars. The name Praesepe (Latin for "manger") goes back to astronomers of antiquity who saw in the two stars near Praesepe two asses eating from a manger, and thus named the stars Asellus Borealis and Asellus Australis. In addition to open star clusters there are globular star clusters (see the constellations Centaurus and Crux, page 76). In open clusters the stars are not as densely packed as in globular ones, which also contain many more stars than the former (up to several million).

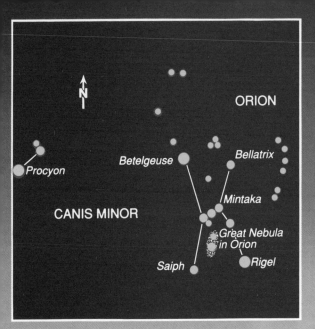

Orion and Canis Minor (the Small Dog)

Orion, which stands for the wild hunter of the same name in Greek mythology, is one of the most impressive constellations in the sky. Especially famous is the Great Nebula in Orion (M 42), a radiant gas cloud in outer space that can be seen on a clear night with the naked eye. By contrast, Canis Minor has only one brilliant star, Procyon. A comparison of the distances from Earth of some of the brightest stars is interesting. Procyon: 11 light-years; Betelgeuse: 470 light-years; Rigel: 1,300 light-years. Yet all three appear to us equidistant from Earth! Our vision is not equipped to register such mind-boggling distances spatially the way our eyes inform us that a house across the street is closer than the mountain in the distance behind it.

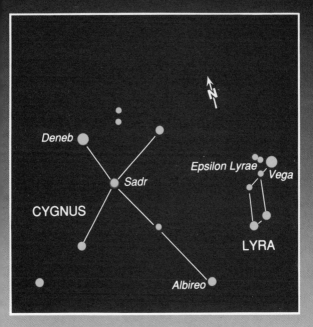

Cygnus (the Swan) and Lyra (the Lyre)

According to Greek myth, Lyra was the musical instrument the famous singer Orpheus played, and Cygnus was the swan in whose guise Zeus approached Leda. Modern astronomy has detected interesting double stars in these two constellations. Two or more stars revolving around a central point of gravity—somewhat similar to the way the planets revolve around our sun—are a rather common phenomenon in outer space. To view the star Albireo in Cygnus it is best to look through a small telescope; Epsilon Lyrae will appear double without magnification to stargazers with keen eyesight.

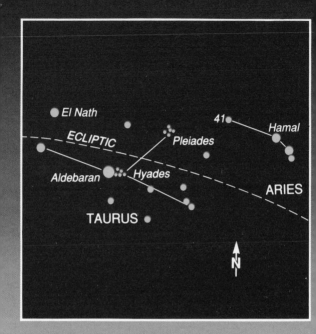

Aries (the Ram) and Taurus (the Bull)

The Pleiades and the Hyades, both in Taurus and clearly visible to the naked eye, are considered the most beautiful star clusters. The Pleiades were named by the Greeks for the seven daughters of the giant Atlas, and they are therefore also known as the Seven Sisters (distance from Earth: 450 light-years). Photographs taken through large telescopes show them in color (see front cover). In connection with the constellation Aries a note on star nomenclature may be in order. Most stars do not have proper names but are designated by a Greek letter or a number, followed by the possessive form of the constellation's Latin name. An example of this is "41 Arietis" in the map above.

Star Map Series S

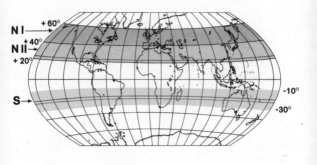

Star Maps and Constellations

The maps in Series S are for the latitudes between 10 to 30 degrees south. Applicable for Brazil, Peru, Bolivia, South Africa, Tanzania, Botswana, Madagascar, Australia, and New Zealand.

Reminders:

Before you use the maps of this series, it is important to remember this directive: When you watch the sky, the letter on the map indicating the direction in which you face must point downward. This means that when you look northward the book will be upside down (see page 16). The familiar constellations of the northern sky then seem to be upside down compared to how we think of them, and the southern sky thus presents a somewhat unfamiliar aspect to observers from the northern half of the globe.

The initials "LMC" and "SMC" used in some of the maps that follow stand for the Large and the Small Magellanic Clouds (see pages 13, 75, and 78). The sky of the southern hemisphere includes many constellations with strange names, such as Antlia, the Air Pump. These constellations were not named until the eighteenth century (see page 11).

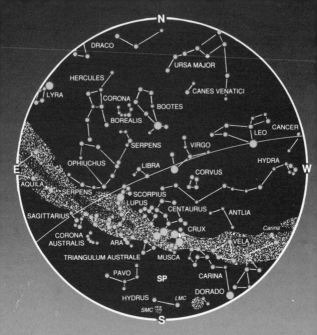

Celestial Events during June

Winter begins in the southern hemisphere. For dates and times, see page 22.
1992: Jupiter is in Leo and visible for about an hour after sunset. (Saturn is visible in Capricorn from 2 AM on. Mars is in Pisces and Aries from 3 AM on.) A partial lunar eclipse is visible on June 15 in South America, the Pacific, and south Atlantic. A total solar eclipse can be seen in the south Atlantic.
1993: Mars is in the western part of Leo, and Jupiter just to the east in Virgo. Their apparent distance from each other continues to shrink and they are joined by Mercury in the evening sky. In the middle of the month, southern observers can see these three for just 45 minutes in the evening sky in Virgo. On June 4 there is a total lunar eclipse visible from eastern Asia and Australia. (Saturn, in Capricorn, rises about 1 AM).
1994: Early in June, Mercury is in Gemini and Taurus. Venus glows ever brighter during the month, setting about three hours after the sun. Jupiter dominates the rest of the evening in Virgo. (Saturn, in Auarius, is visible from about 1 AM on.)

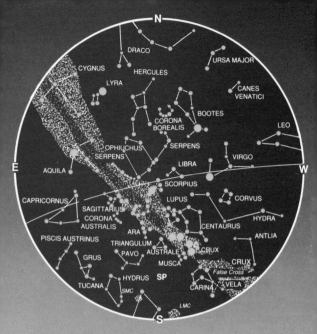

Celestial Events during July

The distance between Earth and the sun is at its annual maximum: 94.3 million miles (152.1 million km). For dates and times, see page 23. Some of the best viewing of the Milky Way and its wonders can be seen from southern latitudes during July and August.

1992: Jupiter is in Leo; Saturn, in Capricorn. (Mars is in Aries and Taurus in the eastern sky from 1 AM on.)

1993: Jupiter, in Virgo, and Mars, in Leo, both set before midnight. Although Jupiter is much farther from Earth than Mars, by July Jupiter's yellowish light has become noticeably brighter than Mars' (Saturn, in Capricorn, is visible from 11 PM on.)

1994: Venus moves out of Leo to join Jupiter in Virgo by the end of the month. Venus is now by far the brightest point of light in the sky. (Saturn, in Aquarius, can be seen through the latter part of the night, rising at about 11 PM. Mars, in Taurus, is visible from 2 AM on.)

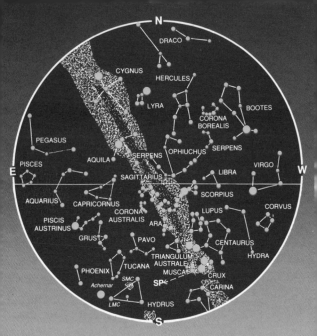

Celestial Events during August

1992: Partial lunar eclipse is visible in Australia, New Zealand, and the Pacific. On August 7, Saturn is in its best viewing position of the year in Capricorn. Early in the month, Jupiter and Venus move ever closer together until lost in the twilight glow by the 15th. (Mars, in Taurus, can be seen from 1 AM on in the eastern sky.)

1993: Saturn appears in the evening sky for the first time this year; on the 14th, it is at opposition, which means it rises at sunset in Capricorn. Jupiter and Mars appear to move closer together during the month, in Virgo. Venus is beginning to appear in the morning sky.

1994: Venus is at its greatest brightness for this year, but Jupiter, to the south, almost matches Venus' brightness this month. Both are in Virgo. Saturn rises in Aquarius just after sunset. (Mars, in Gemini, rises about 1 AM).

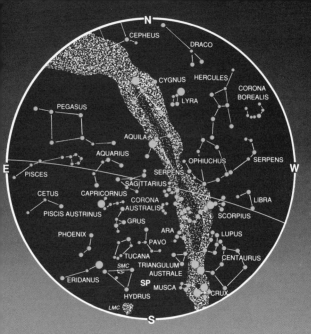

Celestial Events during September

Southern hemisphere spring begins this month. For dates and times, see page 25. See if you can locate the familiar Summer Triangle and the Great Square of Pegasus in the northern part of the sky.

1992: Venus shines as the evening star in the west until about 7:30 PM. Saturn is in Capricorn. (Mars is in Gemini in the eastern sky after 11 PM.)

1993: Mars and Jupiter are in close conjunction on September 7. They appear in the evening sky, only briefly, in Virgo. Saturn remains the planet of the first half of the night. (Venus, in Leo, is now well placed as the "morning star.")

1994: Jupiter and Venus seem to be moving closer together in Libra, but without coming as close together as Mars and Jupiter did last year. Both are visible up to about three hours after sunset in the south. Saturn appears in Aquarius in the evening sky on September 1. During the last two weeks of the month, Mercury appears in a good viewing position.

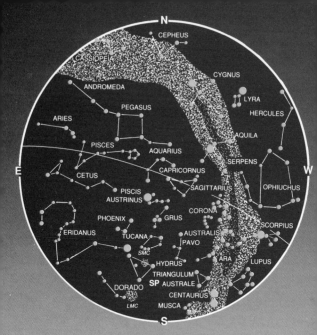

Celestial Events during October

1992: Saturn is in Capricorn; Venus appears for about an hour, until 7 PM, low in the western sky; Mars is in the east in the constellation Gemini from 11 PM on. (The careful observer may catch a glimpse of Jupiter in the morning twilight. It is near the Leo-Virgo border this month.)

1993: In the southern hemisphere, sky watchers have the rare opportunity of seeing a second close conjunction of Mars. Mars and Mercury can be seen together in the evening sky in the constellation Libra.

1994: Jupiter is covered up by the moon on October 7, as seen from the southernmost latitudes of the southern hemisphere. On the night of the 7th Jupiter will appear very close to the moon for northern hemisphere observers. Mercury disappears from the sky during the first week of October, as does Venus in the middle of the month, leaving only Saturn, in Aquarius, to be observed in the evening sky. (Mars, now in Cancer, is visible after 1 AM— midnight once standard time goes back into effect.)

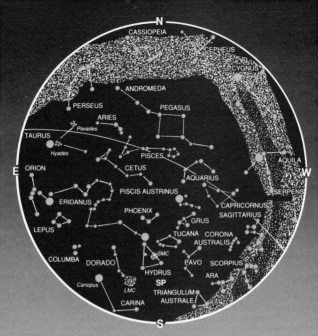

Celestial Events during November

1992: Saturn is in Capricorn, visible most of the night. Mars is in Gemini and rises about 8 PM. Venus, in Sagittarius, is in the western sky until about 7 PM. (Jupiter is in the morning sky from 5 AM on in Virgo.)

1993: On the 6th, a rare transit of Mercury will occur. The tiny planet passes in front of the sun as seen from Earth. On the 13th, a partial solar eclipse will be visible from the southernmost parts of the southern hemisphere. On the 29th, observers in South America can see a total lunar eclipse. (Although Jupiter begins to appear in the morning sky at the end of the month, and Mars may be glimpsed in the early evening at its end, Saturn is the only easily visible planet.)

1994: A solar eclipse can be seen on the 3rd of the month. The path of totality cuts through the middle of South America. Saturn, in Aquarius, is the only planet visible in the evening sky. (Mars, in Leo, rises about 11 PM and can be seen through the rest of the night. Venus begins to appear in the morning near the end of the month.)

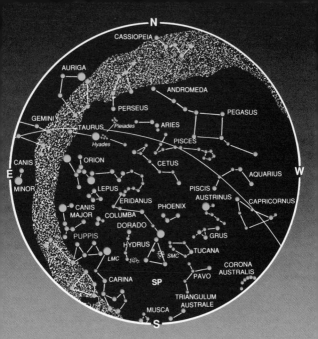

Celestial Events during December

Summer begins on December 21. For exact times, see the beginning of northern hemisphere winter on page 28.

1992: On December 9, there is a total lunar eclipse over Europe, fully visible at midnight in Germany, Austria, and Switzerland. On the 24th, a partial solar eclipse can be seen over the north Pacific. Saturn and Venus appear very close together on the 21st in Capricorn, visible in the western sky until 9 PM; Mars is in Gemini. (Jupiter is in Virgo from 3 AM on.)

1993: This year comes to a close with Saturn the only easily visible planet in the evening sky. It is in the border area between Capricorn and Aquarius, but leaves the sky about 10 PM. (Jupiter is the only other planet visible this month. It rises in Virgo at about 4 AM.)

1994: Saturn, in Aquarius, is the only easily visible planet at sunset, but at 9:30 PM Mars rises in Leo. (Venus is in Libra and rises after 4 AM, followed by Jupiter, in Scorpius, at about 5:30.)

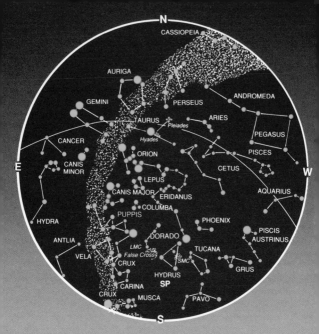

Celestial Events during January

The distance between Earth and the sun is at its annual minimum: only 91.2 million miles (147.1 million km). For each year's data and time, see page 29. Watch out for the "false cross," which bears some resemblance to the Southern Cross!

1993: Venus is the "evening star," appearing in the west for a few hours in Aquarius. Mars is in Gemini. (Jupiter rises about 1 AM in Virgo.)

1994: Saturn can be seen in the west after sunset all month, setting a few hours later. By the end of the month, Mercury joins Saturn very low in the evening sky, so Saturn can be used as a guide to finding the elusive innermost planet. (Jupiter, in Libra, rises after 2 AM.)

1995: Mercury and Saturn are again visible in the evening sky. Saturn can be seen the entire month in Aquarius. One may catch a glimpse of Mercury in Capricorn around the 15th. Mars rises in the late evening. (Jupiter and Venus rise about two hours before the sun in Scorpius.)

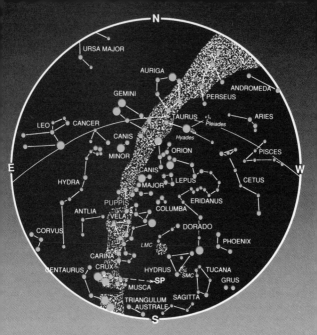

Celestial Events during February

The south celestial pole, marked "SP," can be found by extending the line formed by the central axis of the Southern Cross as shown near the bottom of the map. This may be the best way to get your bearings in the southern sky, which doesn't have a convenient "Pole Star." The Large and Small Magellanic Clouds are well placed for viewing during the winter months.

1993: Mars, in Gemini, and Venus, in Pisces, dominate the early evening sky, but Venus is very low by the end of the month. Jupiter rises before midnight in Virgo.

1994: Mercury and Saturn start the month low in the western sky at sunset, but quickly disappear in the evening twilight. (Jupiter is now in Libra and can be seen after midnight.)

1995: While Saturn quickly disappears from the evening sky, Mars returns. It is directly opposite the sun on February 12 and on that date rises at sunset. (Jupiter rises after 3 AM in Scorpius.)

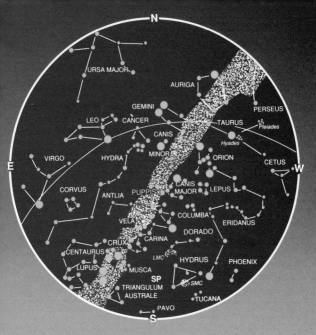

Celestial Events during March

Fall officially begins in the southern hemisphere at the same time spring does in the north. In the Eastern Time Zone, this occurs on March 20 at 9:41 AM in 1993, on the 20th at 3:28 PM in 1994, and on the 20th at 9:14 PM in 1995.

1993: Mars, still in Gemini, is the only planet easily visible at sunset. Jupiter appears at about 9 PM in Virgo at the beginning of the month and rises earlier and earlier each night.

1994: No planets are visible in the early evening. (By the time Jupiter rises in Libra, it is already past 11 PM. The morning, however, brings an impressive grouping of Mars, Saturn, and Mercury to the predawn southern sky.)

1995: Mars is quite bright in the constellations Cancer and Leo this month. (Jupiter, in Capricorn, and Mercury, in Aquarius, are easy to spot in the morning sky.)

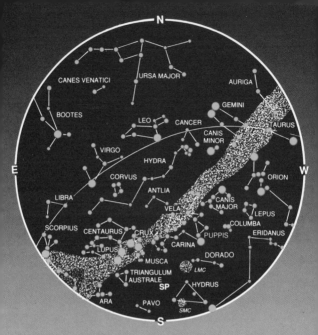

Celestial Events during April

1993: Jupiter and Mars dominate the evening sky. Mars is the farther west, in Gemini. Jupiter is in Virgo. (Saturn rises just before sunrise in Aquarius.)

1994: Venus begins to appear as the "evening star." The night of the 12th to the 13th, the moon passes in front of Venus as seen from the high Arctic latitudes. From all other areas it will appear very close to Venus—a pretty sight. Jupiter is well placed after 10 PM and can be seen the rest of the night in Libra. (Saturn rises shortly before sunrise in Aquarius.)

1995: There is a partial eclipse of the moon visible on the night of April 15, and an annular solar eclipse on the 29th, visible from Central and South America. The planets visible this month are Mars in Cancer (Jupiter, in Scorpius, in the morning sky, and a close grouping of Venus and Saturn just before sunrise.)

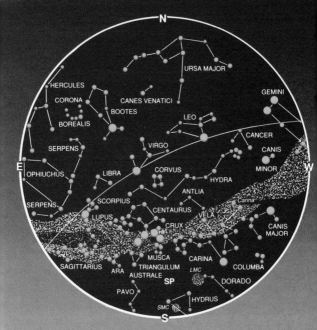

Celestial Events during May

1993: Mars, in Cancer, and Jupiter, in Virgo, continue in the evening sky. Both are well placed for early evening viewing. (Saturn is moving into the normal sky now, rising about one hour before the sun.)

1994: Venus grows brighter and higher in the evening sky. By the time it sets, Jupiter is high enough in the sky to be easily observed in Libra. On May 10, an annular solar eclipse can be seen throughout most of North, Central, and South America. Maximum eclipse and partial phases can be seen at southern latitudes throughout much of South America.

1995: Mars is in the evening sky in Leo all month and is joined briefly by tiny Mercury. In the middle of the month, this planet nearest the sun can be seen by the careful northern hemisphere observer in the northwestern sky just after sunset. Jupiter becomes visible about 10 PM, in Scorpius. (Saturn, in Aquarius, rises about 4 AM. On the 22nd, the rings of Saturn are edge-on as seen from earth, so even in larger telescopes, they are not visible.)

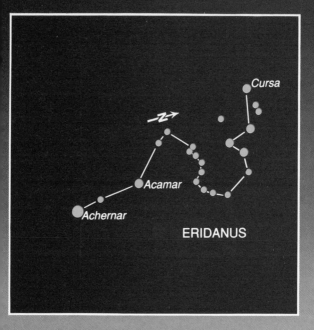

Eridanus

You may notice that in this picture the arrow pointing north is in an almost horizontal position rather than in a more or less vertical one. We had to draw Eridanus in this position because otherwise it would not have fit the format of the illustrations. Eridanus is one of the longest constellations in the sky, extending from Orion almost to the south pole (indicated in star maps by the letters SP). Eridanus has one star that deserves special mention: Achernar, one of the brightest stars in the southern celestial hemisphere. It is 78 light-years distant from Earth. In Greek mythology Eridanus is a river that figures in many stories, and the stars that make up this constellation form a curvy line across the sky that resembles a meandering river.

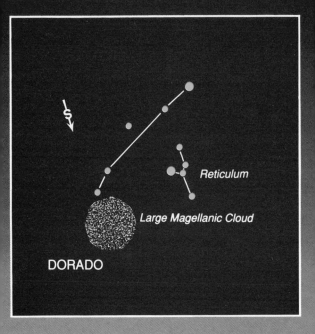

Dorado

The constellation Dorado was first identified by the German astronomer Johann Bayer in 1603. Within its confines there is a truly "golden" heavenly object: the Large Magellanic Cloud (see color photo on page 13). It is today a major focus of scientific research conducted at observatories located in the southern hemisphere. Because it is so close to Earth, it appears as the brightest and most impressive galaxy outside of the Milky Way. It is composed of 18 to 20 billion stars and is removed from us by 160,000 light-years. The Large Magellanic Cloud is clearly visible to the unaided eye—even at full moon!

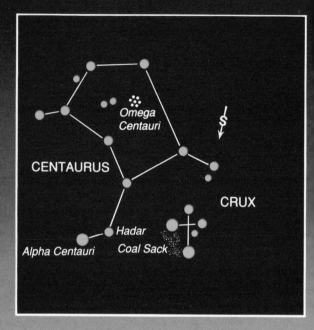

Crux (the Southern Cross) and Centaurus

Here we are contemplating one of the most beautiful, star-studded regions of the sky. The famous Southern Cross (Crux) was used as a guide by sailors of earlier ages to establish the points of the compass on the high seas, for the central axis of the cross points toward the south celestial pole (SP) (see maps S/February and S/August on pages 70 and 64). The Coalsack, one of the darkest spots in the beautiful, luminous band of the Milky Way, is located in the area of the Southern Cross. Here dense dust clouds, acting like a wall block the view to the stars beyond them. Toliman in the constellation Centaurus, also known as Alpha Centauri, is the closest star to Earth—4.2 light-years or 25 trillion miles (40 trillion km) away. Omega Centauri is the brightest globular star cluster in the sky.

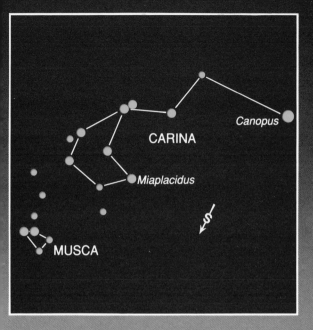

Carina (the Keel) and Musca (the Fly)

One of the most exciting Greek myths tells about the ship Argos and the heroic feats accomplished by its crew, the Argonauts. No wonder that the gods elevated this legendary ship to the heavens. It took up a large area below Canis Major and Orion—indeed, too large an area according to modern astronomy, which regards constellations as nothing more than a useful device for subdividing the sky. Argo Navis has therefore been cut up into three sections: Puppis (the Poop), Vela (the Sail), and Carina. Carina contains Canopus, the second brightest star in the sky. A star of superlatives, Canopus shines 20,000 times more brightly than the sun and is 60 times its size. Its distance from Earth is 370 light-years.

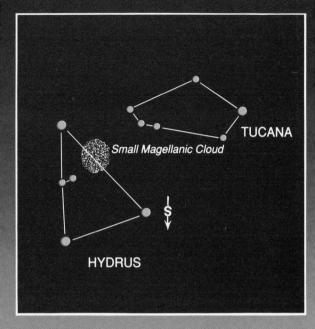

Hydrus (the Small Water Snake) and Tucana (the Toucan)

The sky of the southern hemisphere is especially rich in exotic names for constellations. One example is Tucana, which is the name of a South American bird family. Hydrus, which is next to Tucana, contains one of the most interesting objects of the southern sky, namely, the Small Magellanic Cloud. This cloud was discovered by Ferdinand Magellan, who was the first to sail around the world in the years 1519 to 1522. The Small and the Large Magellanic Clouds (see Constellation Dorado on page 75 and the color photo on page 13), are our closest galactic neighbors, being "a mere" 160,000 light-years away from us. There, many million stars combine in formations that are similar to our Milky Way Galaxy. The Small Magellanic Cloud can be seen only from the southern hemisphere, but from there it is visible to the naked eye.